ALSO BY JONATHAN FAIA

Wylde Serenity

LOVE LETTERS
from
BARSTOW

JONATHAN FAIA

ARCHWAY
PUBLISHING

Archway Publishing books may be ordered through booksellers or by contacting:

Archway Publishing
1663 Liberty Drive
Bloomington, IN 47403
www.archwaypublishing.com
844-669-3957

ISBN: 978-1-6657-2464-7 (sc)
ISBN: 978-1-6657-2465-4 (e)

Library of Congress Control Number: 2022910251

Print information available on the last page.

Archway Publishing rev. date: 06/13/2022

DEDICATED

Though we can go through life feeling ignored and with empty souls, you always have your dreams. Some of us continue to lose sleep, spending long nights fighting with racing thoughts and it's alright. I'm glad you're strong enough to still be here. For those who are no longer here, it's important that you know that you're missed, even though we may have never met. These words are for every heart that's died a little to feel love, and for those that continue to. We're all a beautiful composition of broken. Thank you to the public library, for without you I couldn't be a storyteller, I'd still just be a dreamer.

BREAD AND WINE

If mistakes become regrets, I'll be there in an hour

Sometimes, you only have one chance to feel lightning bolts in the daytime

Taking every opportunity to fill up on emptiness

Who doesn't want to feel a little cheaper than they need to?

Regret between two people who speak the same language

It's a kinship and affinity

It's in the character of your sins

It's social distortion

Collecting tries like trophies, my heart only felt safe in storms

Leaving life to become a necessary inconvenience

Spending days comparing imperfect loves to perfect potential

We all breathe it in

It's smiles that make us weak

ADHESIVE

Trapped in a life with no beginning

Chasing my whiskey spinning wheel

Blood alas, boiling among back door frenzied deals

I want to be the salt of your skin

I can be the vapor of your angel being

Together we're a striking match, with the world as our fire

I wish I could show you what you think I'm made of

Jonathan Faia

ALL THAT WALKS BESIDE ME

All I have walks beside me

Sheltered cumulus endings to streets lined with juniper garland

Strangers walk by, brushing upon you their naked aggression

Stories never told allow a passerby to disappear into golden sins

Is that me?

Would that make me too normal for you?

I get the feeling you'll walk away

I wish I could be everything you wanted all the time

Dulled and made thick with sleet in my heart, how can I lift you up?

Any opportunity you could afford, a missing heart would allow me
to live

The heavy freeze in the complex pavement of my being would
be thawed

ANSWERING MACHINE

I wish I could breathe life into a letter

I call to hear your voice weeks after you've left

Fledgling spirit longing for a message

I call when you're not home because I'd never be able to say goodnight

Trying to find the courage to say I love you to your
answering machine

I don't speak because it's easier than admitting I was wrong

You are my something better

But I've already settled for less

Jonathan Faia

BALLAD OF THE REGULARS

Everyone wants to be special here

Those who dream live to become doubters

Chasing demons born into yesterday

Looking down the railing of a bar in jealous curiosity

Inspiring tomorrow's marvelous madness

BELIEVE

I want you to believe in life

Even when you feel like giving up

The world can be a beautiful place if you have a hand to hold

Believing is hearing the angels sing, even while suffering

I want you to believe in life, even when I don't

Let your courage be your crown

Jonathan Faia

BORN TO LOSE

Cocaine fame, blessed in the midnight score

Lives left chasing lust on the interstate

Waking hate in the morning, passing hate around noon

No remorse or regret

Living a life yet nothing to do

Paving the road with scars that bear one's name

Everyone has scars

Find the person who believes yours are beautiful

CAN I TELL YOU

There is no eternal blessing or reward for wasting the dawn

Missing in a wet labyrinth of kisses

Some moments in life are not designed to be understood

Instead, we should just let them be what they are

Miracles

Nobody knows the secrets of pre-eternity

CARRY ME HOME

In the East, the crescent moon lies low

Hanging like a wise jewel on a silvery thread

Even the loneliest of stars have their place in tow

Playing games in the infinite darkness overhead

Do you have a favorite song?

While the hills and lights begin to geld in a grand symphony, I finally got you where I want you

Glistening glimmer, the perfect balance of music and silence

Listening to the sounds of darkness, dividing God's plan for eternity

It's a homecoming

Don't let life compromise your star

CHANGELING

There is a light we can't always be

People look at you differently, maybe someone you used to know

Where did you go, and why did you change?

They miss the old you and maybe you do too

Missing the things that gave you smiles, and laughter that seem a world away

It used to be so easy waiting to bloom

You've become more

We no longer have to hide our wept faces of desire

Jonathan Faia

COLONIZATION

Your water is warm, but who knows how deep

Your confidence has no elemental center

It forces me to swallow the words I longed for a lifetime to share

Your facade is true existence

Lit from a fire beneath you, you let no man in

I have mourned, while other times I've held constant vigil awaiting a crack in the armor of opportunity

A hero is waiting for you

One who will shoulder your world's burdens

One who will colonize your every emotion

One who sees you as home

CRYING

Wounded and black-eyed for your approval

Porcelain skin, lily-white over the skies of West Hollywood

Below the wet sidewalks lives the open side of my best friend

Before they became still in the face, they raised the skies

Eyes left crying like a burning manger

Raising their cares to the wild skies a thunder

Lonely in gray, a bitter wave once tossed

Found lonely under the edge of night

We are the ones whose hope is young

Jonathan Faia

DAYS OF THE WEEK

I constantly remember you

Remember you as you were in the Autumn of 1993

Your calm heart over a sea of green and white

A sunset waiting for permission in your eyes

A tree's falling leaves floating into the puddles in my heart

Thoughts of you becoming vertiginous memories in my soul

Why do your eyes voyage away just like they did that Autumn?

In my mind, we share kisses that leave embers in their wake

My every breath is a letter to you

DEEP

If I were to lose you, I'd certainly lose myself

Searching for things to hold dear I was never able to find it in myself

Feeling broken forced me to focus on prayer

Your love came as deep as any ocean

Who chose to hear me?

Complexities in life create games that few can win

That doesn't stop life from playing

Hearts leaning askew may die but the entirety lives on

But you allow me to see it's where faith resides

It's another kind of serenity, another kind of hangover

DHARMA PUNKS

"Gen X" punks posing as the enlightened

Flannelled in adaptability, they are young and restless

At 19, I contemplated becoming a Buddhist

Saving me from the belly of my experience

Remove me from my genocide

My poems don't delight me

Instead, I cruise worn out barstools in desperation at last call

So, what if there is enlightenment

I'll pass

I have too much angst about missing the Beat Revolution

Rather I sit here contemplating what cause to take as the antithesis
to excess

It's Tuesday where's the revolution?

My weakness is my mundane diurnal silence

It helps me forget that nobody will read this and that I'm creating for
creation's sake

Sit boldly America, you are about to be forgotten

For you are the sons of no one

DOLL PARTS

Clad in Doc Martens and blue bangs

I can feel your heart crying

Inhaling your spirit, sighing

Picking up conversations from deep in your imagination

I can answer all your lonely voices

Until then, my name will be might have been

I don't know where we're going but I'd like to be by your side

We can stay out and watch for sunsets until I become your truth

Jonathan Faia

EMPTY BOTTLE

I live life yet I'm a bottle full of empty stories

Not the divine sense of emptiness found in a Hermann Hesse novel

The emptiness coiled in cold envy, waiting to be discovered

A lifetime gorging on life's excess

Is this what it is to achieve?

Emptiness; a hole?

In this world do I even exist?

Even in accomplishment, there's nothing

I know emptiness, and I have nothing to say

No reason to move on

The nights I've built a slumber don't transcend into anything but sweat-soaked bedcovers

I know emptiness and I'll be generous in its sharing

FIRE

Fire is more than the idea of the flame

It is the blooming petal of the whitest orchid birthed from the Sun's radiance

Burning away the once glorious heap sat at each bedside

Soiled in guilt for atrocities committed on one's heart

Fire is the vanity that gathers at your insides in public

Fire is the soot formed relations left in failure's way

Fire may be the last of the world's greatest unstructured paradigms

Induced by a mind's loose oxidation

Cauterizing emotions

Forcing the creation of needs and wants

Jonathan Faia

HORNETS

Who derived the notion that we owe this world anything?

Why do we need to explain ourselves?

Maybe we think too much about too much

Sometimes the more we do what is right, the more we feel further apart

The problem is the notion that we know what's right

We don't know anything

We know what our junior college education told us

The modern-day playground for amateur philosophers and middle-class intellectuals

Knowledge is failure

Failing in study and failing in life

All we owe the world is our failures

For failure is enlightenment's education

HOUSE OF BROKEN LOVE

Why do we choose broken people?

Is it because the world is full of them?

Broken individuals feeling their way through broken lives

Fumbling like a drunk who falls over their nightstand after a long night out

Filling love's begging bowls

We sit at love's table

Feasting on broken holiness

One thread holding us together

We're all looking for broken love

Jonathan Faia

HUNT BRANCH

Why are libraries cradled in fear?

Books lying on the floor

Segregated on a whim

Unsteady but reliable stacks of lore

Perennially lost in the sea of transient vessels looking for refuge

A place where life can become yours

Adult shadow play that can summon your deepest sense of adolescence

Slamming the doors on risible stereotypes

Weeping as words fall from the pages in silence

Fear is a formal matter, prematurely bestowed on the illness of life's ruin

One small gesture in the span of corridors and dead ends

Bibliographic cults, spiraling staircases of knowledge one tattered cover at a time

Always pointing to the Sun, answering every question

HYMNS AND HALLELUJAHS

From chaos to hymns and halleluiahs

Her silhouette owns real estate in your mind

She's your favorite mistake

Your favorite word

Truly a life's work

Once the oxygen that gave a popper life

She's the ghost living in your head

I WAS WRONG

The misconception in life is that you think you own love forever

Show them how important they are

Act like now is special

Don't spend your smiles chasing the past

INTERMISSION

Life is both beginning and end

Memories are our intermission

In between, we just barter for affirmation

INVISIBILITY

I've met all my promises at sundown as I hold on to the thread

Piercing my vale of anonymity

Invisible in a tangible world

I've found a sickness in me

No place for my body within my own mind

My spirit should be beautiful

I give in to wondering by the day

Wondering what went wrong, why do I feel a breed apart

Struggling constantly, pandering to midnight negotiations in my mind

Where is the marvel in it all?

KISS ME

Pulling you into me, we kiss

The type of kiss that pulls the soul out of you

The type of kiss where you can inhale the magic in your partner

Drowning in the essence of laughter even in the pits of your stomach

The essence that produces smiles

The type of smile that permeates your idea of what the world can be

An essence that lets you remember what it's like to love

Really love someone

Burning love that's difficult to survive

That type of kiss

LAZY HEARTS

Lazy hearts dressed for a homecoming disguised as Earth in July

Stirring echoes of promises once made

A man can lose his mind without his art which can be taken
at anytime

Art may be the only thing that can set a man's soul free to fly

Art is love

Chasing art, I'm fatigued

Minds ache in the wake of racing thoughts

It's overwhelming, mass pursuit

The art I deserve only brings more of what I don't want

MIRACLE NUMBER TWO

Living life as a flower feeling a slow burn

Living is not easy

Don't be caught saving yourself from the dirt

I'm not looking for heroes

I'm not looking for anything

Miracles find me dancing with lies

The same miracles looking to save a life

Miracles welcoming silence under the shadows of the still

Traveling roads of emotional violence, I lost myself along the way

Burning gardens at their best and burying broken dreams

Jonathan Faia

MOTIVATION

Motivated by the lack of doubt, the world writes letters to cry

The thorns are the best part of us

Life, like Winter

Hearts feel bruised, waking to a hand scarred by splinters

I'm seeking the same

Any way the pleasure comes

I will always stand by your side in company

I will forever love the loneliest parts of you

OMISSION

Vacated is the world

It claims the space from here to her

Where can we find a conscience in this world?

Artificial words become vessels free from volunteers

Vessels that make it hard to hold victims from their tears

If I tune in for your song, will it give way to the shotgun that is
my Sun?

Spinning and blinded; this world goes on

MESSAGE

Staying home at night trying to breathe letters into life

Surviving on clueless hope feels like I will never feel again

Death-defying confessions are left waiting at your feet

Trying to find the courage to say I love you

You are my something better

But where can we go if I've already settled for less

A single book of matches couldn't burn what is standing my way

Please bury all my pictures and tell the world I was okay

If my message was forgotten, then at least remember it for today

PASADENA

"I'm going to push away", she said in Pasadena the night before

Sitting alone, dreaming right from wrong

Contemplating an end, something more eternal

A heart all alone left bleeding in circumstance

Even in eternity we are all looking for a home

I hung up, she called back, it's the way our process always started

Inside I knew that was the finality of what she felt that night

Everything I see is a constant reminder of her

Sending me drifting out of the present to a place where only memories
run nostalgia

Leaves me standing in wet grass, pulled out into the undertow
of regret

My new home

Jonathan Faia

PLEASE DON'T GO

Please don't leave before I get better

My soul has worth

Hushed promises of love and dreams

Whispers of love only come out in the dark

Turn your whispers into a riot

Memories are all I can feel

I dream of you drinking in the sunshine because you never liked the taste of rain

In case I forget to say it, I'm sorry

I hope you find your chapel in the sun

PROVERBS

Don't spend your life trying to fulfill perfect potential

Only compare yourself to you

RUNNING

Soulmates never let you run alone, they run alongside you

Side by side in mistakes and bliss

You are two people sharing one story

Walking along the open road of love and life

Soulmates are those who understand and live the struggle

Don't settle for a lover

Soulmates will walk the same fire and razor's edge

What's important is recognizing when you find them

Sometimes their time with us is but moments, while mistakes feel everlasting

Let your moments last a lifetime

SCARECROW

In a land where scarecrows beg for anonymity can a soul be set free
to fly?

Begging questions in a world where destruction is creation

Figures are constantly seen leaning, twisted in the wind

A shadow's shape surpasses all messages and meaning

Hope suspended over nothingness

Disappearing in faith and want delivering empty letters to
hollow hearts

SKIES

Skies filled with vast and solemn clusters of moisture wakening upon a soft subtle glimpse of dusk

Wakening upon the Sun's demise; Lit but fading

Cooling temperatures of a vindictive essence rain down as
night appears

Longing to be the voice of the voiceless

Shouting at the heavens with reverence but words won't come out

Peerless power engulfs my being

Drinking in desperation as a concession

Eyes lost wide open

SLUMBERS

Suicide has got my head wrapped around you

Setting my soul in darkness

With the hopes that I'll sleep in perfect light

You were my today

You're my last day of Summer

Jonathan Faia

STROLLING WITH DOUBT

It's generous the way we let words devour us

Never wanting to listen but always letting them in

It's our favorite routine, our primary cycle

In honor, we let our attractions slowly kill us

Our simple attraction to everything that hurts

Letting those things, we hold dear destroy us

Define us

Holding us close enough to make us feel alive

SWAY

I love to watch you sway

You give me eternity despite me

Jonathan Faia

SWIM WITH ME

Born void of innocence

I need to walk away but not today

I swim beyond the channels that divide the paths upon which we
might have met

Building a fortress on a house of cards, that transformed into
a reservoir

Bathing in your tears

Atop the menacing crest of anger, it's just you and me

Together we can find an inner soul worth saving

Put away my grave

Youth proved that the channel changed the first time you saw
my blood

Alone and broken

Today we bleed together and the wounds will heal

SYNCHRONICITY

Synchronicity is life's promise of truth

Parallels haunting us outside of time

Finding coincidence in abstract events

Taxing a logical mind

Synchronicity can be thoughtful

Reminiscent of events, periods, and vodka fueled decisions

Blind eyes will pass

Allowing synchronicity to move in favor of more deserving shadows

Jonathan Faia

SYNONYMS

Sit back and watch my end

I've wasted six years here

My life decaying, my promise lying a blank

My words are often left disconnected

Feverishly scribbling my life away on napkins and yellow legal pads

My lips longing to do penance

Searching for life's synonyms

THE CROWS OF CAROL DRIVE

In a world where heroes are legends, some silently fly by

Cruising the city nights on foot without a cape

Waiting for opportunities to spiral away from the gray landscape

Dark streets lined with the dying trees encapsulated by a rundown post office

Crowned on its corner with a 6 AM tavern filled with beer gutters and disappointment

The flickering skyline was a compromise to what darkness illuminated a neighborhood's being

Stars did not twinkle here

A block born of outcasts

The crows look to drink from those gutters before perching themselves high above on dim streetlights

Regret can be such an understatement

Jonathan Faia

THE MEETING

I've always been inside you; don't you feel we should meet?

I made it my life's work to give you everything

I cut my fingers crossing my heart with promises

You make me feel a lifetime in your eyes

You're my poetry

PERFECT STORM

Shining down beneath the sweaty dance hall lights

You see your world

A life so sound, your eyes glisten in her saintly presence

Her heart, A friend made enemy

With a leap and a pause

You've been caught

Too feeble to move on

Straining just to breathe

She has you holding on for another time and place

The true fault is in your stars

For every moment you spend with her you feel like anything
is possible

She became the storm that allowed you to feel safe

TIME

I thought I could create my reflection in the heart of a blind eye

Only to find lying images of untruths

Breaking ties with fading ripples supplied with time

Giving only what I got leaves you asking for everything

Not willing to spare pieces of me

With my time fleeting I have yet to sing my one true song or write that great sonnet

Time has stolen my courage

A glimpse of my mirror image tells no tales, but time lost

BEFORE

To those, I put through hell

Left to walk through my distorted level of perception

Broken hearts

Broken trusts

Just know, I died a little each day learning how to deal with it

It was never you

Lost, deranged, and forgotten, it all encapsulated in my thoughts

I was the one who went mad

I was the fallen traveler who failed to sleep but always dreamed

It was never you, I could not be understood

Even though we sank into each other, it was me who made you feel like you were drowning

Believe me when I say I dreamt of saving us

Jonathan Faia

TSOUKALOS

The stars can be life past, present, and future

I don't sing to the stars, but rather have become indifferent

Stars giving birth to life

While no man standing alone equals greatness, a space lit flame knows better

Without greed, showing nothing but greatness

Sweet thing ecstasies

Have you found your following?

Standing high above a stone untouched by man, stars are starved prophets

Faith has been broken, whispers they cry

Feed us delicately in peace

Stars are a lonely ocean, plowing God's field

WAITING IN LINE

He's been waiting a lifetime for you

Just as you've dreamt of him

Burry your cathedrals

Sanctioned by ever long constellations

This is where you'll blur your line

Let your journey be that voyage of discovery we all dream of

Jonathan Faia

WALK AWAY

Heaven was only half right that night

She was a sonnet

But she wouldn't remember me, not even for a day

Instead, I spend every day longing for her to be the darkness between my stars

JUMP ROPE GAZERS

If we walk hand in hand with silence, will we eclipse the Sun?

Our hearts have been known to surrender to violence

Here's another time I won't be your hero

All my life I dreamt of being, just being

Unfulfilled dreams have built my everything

Jonathan Faia

WET SAND

Creation's color fades into the wet empty sand

Loving by mystery

Weakening the will

Golden suns leaking brightness on a soft cinnamon brow

Missing all things good to the touch

Fading into the essence of life

Forcing the masses to cripple in the wake of every pass

Leaving pulverous destruction upon their exit

Finding a final state of an impeccant spirit in light

I miss you

WOULD

You heal my secondhand living

All I ever got from you was whatever I could take

Your essence makes me want to heal, while your words make me want to cry

I'm stuck waiting at the door with feeble dreams of American Bandstand

I'd die to make you mine

Jonathan Faia

YESTERDAY, DREAMS

I'd like to go back to yesterday

I don't want to know what tomorrow will bring

The sky burns red but blasphemous

Stars don't shine anymore

I'm left chasing holy myths

Never realizing the cost or the toll it takes on your body and spirit

I can't write my poem until I'm in my right mind

Yesterday was angelic, it was the most human of sin

Yesterday was a dream

YOU MAKE ME FEEL
THREE GLASSES IN

I'm still wondering if you were real because I've been known to get it wrong

Your memory visits often

Mostly when I'm sitting alone in the dark

You should know that your heart still beats in me

You make my world move a little slower

There is no sign of the Sun without you

My heart can't feel sober with thoughts of you

I've staggered and fallen, but have never been able to feed my illusions of us

I let them feed on me

I lose control with every passing sip

Jonathan Faia

ON A DARE

What if you could spend your day thinking of how the world
would end?

Pale shades of blue gasping for life with the Earth left upside on
a whim

Remembering it as if it was yesterday but uncertain; maybe it wasn't

It's possible this was always our life

I'm not sure I even know you now or if I ever really did

As bad as things seem, I'm constantly reminded of what drew me here

Then I begin to ask life's questions

Would your hair still look black under a waning sun?

What's the meaning of the dark between stars?

Why do you say it with less conviction now?

If only I thought of the right words, because your regret is
an understatement

TRUE

If you asked her, she'd tell you she hadn't slept in 13 days

She's built a life on lies

She's good at it and she knows it

She lies when she feels

She lies without speaking

She's lied to the world

If you asked her, she'd say I Love You

Jonathan Faia

CANADIAN CLUB

The first time it happened, it was a dim October

I had turned 21 for the third time

I wasn't very cold, but I desperately wanted to be numb

I succumbed to a long, tall bottle of Canada's finest twelve-dollar whiskey

I added three cubes of ice and when that didn't work, I reached for a chalky fistful of white tablets

An hour in and it felt like, Darkness of the Edge of Town was playing on repeat

I began to shiver and fell asleep, content that I had accomplished enough

I tried to die thirteen times, but I've only succeeded twice

SUGAR

Saturday holds only small pieces of truth, whispering on a whim

Lighting a hazy window, for a short moment of clarity

The wind makes you nervous

You don't know what you do

You complicate things

All while your eyes hold like watercolors, burning a moonbeam blue

These are simple things, let your heart feel

In quiet times let your heart sing

Jonathan Faia

STOCKTON

Once you lit a soul aflame

Giving way to a valiant spectacle, one that rivaled Hell itself

The stabbing, throbbing pain from that flame vastly different from the satisfaction of a dull razor blade

You made me weary, and longing for a heart's reckless abandon

ALL THINGS PASS

Bricks are heavy, so what's your excuse for returning all my secrets?

Did the burden prove too much for you?

Your logic couldn't keep me from crying

You left shoving all my thoughts back into my arms, wishing me a happy life

As my arms grow tired, I'll dream to die a little death

THINGS

It seems a lost mystery to me

We had greed and on that, we could agree

We built a life on the thought we had to want more to be free

Why did lonely become a thing?

FAITHFUL

You shine like a sun

My only friend

Because I believe in you my soul can rest

PAPER DREAMS

It's funny you called me tonight

Our words seemed to always be trapped in a box that we promised to open one day

Jars of I-owe-yous and paper hearts took the place of what we wished we'd said

We'd drifted apart a lifetime ago

Though we stayed bandaged hand in hand

Why do we keep acting like we can't afford to lose each other?

You're a hand that keeps trying to squeeze my heart

From a distance, we're just shapes and lies

PIECES

We were good people once, just failing at it now

The less you think about it the happier you are

Sometimes it just gets hard to hide it well

Once the only light I could see, you shine alone now

The only chattering left are the overlapping voices of yesterday

Leaving only a glimpse of what was, and the ghosts of what should have been our tomorrow

WHY NOT ME

What is it that makes you love him?

Is it the way his love lets you down?

Maybe it's the way he is incapable of lifting your spirit

If you only knew how much my heart breaks when he shatters
your confidence

If only you could see that you're my beautiful composition of broken

PASTEL KINGDOM

You can't be like the other ones

I know it's you

I spend my nights pretending you thought more of me

I wish you held my hand

When you touch me, I remember what it means to feel okay

I STILL TALK ABOUT YOU

We settle for being life's lonely ones

Spending every breath trying to be everyone to someone who doesn't know we're there

It's easier to feel terrified rather than complete

So scared we settle and accept being broken

The real fear is feeling whole

HARDLY GETTING OVER IT

If you only knew how many times, I went on living when I felt like I couldn't anymore

Jonathan Faia

HEARTACHES AND LULLABIES

The first one we love is also the one who teaches us the most
about pain

We start vulnerable and beautiful

Blissfully unaware of heartache

Then with uncalloused hearts, we caress each other's untouched skin

My heart smiled when she walked by

She was radiant in a crowd of grey

Then one day our silences cease to be compatible

Radiance becomes indifference

Then the realization hits, all the while we were flirting with a grave
that looked like love

SOUTH OF SILENCE

We're somewhere south of silence

Placing labels of forever on temporary people

So young to be this hurt

Teens playing adults with no examples of how to love

No one can prepare you for this version of disappointment

It's what happens when you fall in love before you're ready

Jonathan Faia

SHADOWS

I choose seclusion over expectations because I've failed so many times

After midnight reading old messages, sitting alone in the rubble that used to be my moon

Haunted by everything we didn't become

FRUSTRATION INCORPORATED

I want to live my life on the pages of your heart's tale

Far away from the words that force me to save myself

Jonathan Faia

COME UNDONE

I'd like to hitchhike to another moon

One void of constitutions unwound

A place where conversations light a room, and your essence breathes
life in one steadfast swoop

In a life where I've substituted substance for instance, retrospect speaks
to me the same as intentions

When you're far I have to be reminded to breathe, my happenstance
becomes multifaceted

Innocuously leading me to a place where I've always been meant to fall

Finding faith in what's right before my eyes

ROSARY DREAMS

Everything about you hangs over me like a rosary

With twinkling desperation, the idea of you falling asleep with me side by side solidifies my allegiance

If I ever saw you on the street, I'd spend my life dreaming of you starting tonight

NEW

Nothing about your criticism is silent

But it doesn't stop you from exaggerating your influence on my only attempt at art

I try giving silence to my anger

You're wrong and always have been

My shortcomings are mine

They're my muse

I just want someone to know who I am

WITHOUT ORDER

Sitting at home on a Richard Ashcroft type of night, I wonder if we're ever going to learn to fly?

Our shadows left crouching, hiding in the depths of our spirit, darkening our eye's stars

In the disappointing silence of life, what's your redeeming harmony?

Who will be the reason for the idea of your sunbeam smiles?

Sometimes you have to learn the hard way that holding on to everything isn't always what it seems

Life isn't always literature

Jonathan Faia

ESSENCE OF YOU

Your essence looks like rain, taking its first breath of life

You're endless and effortless at the same time

You are what I wish reminded me of me

With a flinching heart, I try so hard to understand the things you see in me

I often feel I'm crying for love, but humming in vain

My restless heartbeat is left tickled over silent petals of your wonder

CELEBRITY SKIN

When you spend a lifetime praying for an end it's hard to grow old wishing you could live forever

Desires descend into the boulevard's body of fire

I hope my legacy can be pictures formed from words

If anything has remained the same, it's the fact that I'm still a glorious mess

The truth still hurts

I've spent the last week in an argument with my ego and soul trying to reach a compromise

I can't seem to stand my own mind

I've seen it all through someone else

Uncelebrated; disturbed, and seldom seen

Jonathan Faia

HUMILIATION STREET

Words often fall out of my wallet but it's not currency widely accepted

Say hello to Humiliation Street

Saying yes to others with eyes filled with protest and false smiles

Having any type of expectation of reciprocation would ruin me

Feelings then become blurred in a frenzy of social certainty
and sunlight

I can't provide you with illustrations but it's there

Failed poets paying for exposure, where are the thinkers?

They are firmly gripping the handle of America's mop

A city block where the only true visionaries make sense when off
their meds

I WALK ALONE

I walk alone so I don't have to say I'm sorry

It was never your fault

Darkness moves me

Holding on to promises of tomorrow that never come

I walk alone because I don't believe in forgiveness

But it doesn't stop me from dreaming of the clouds

IGNITION

The morning gray ignites those twisted in shapes and melancholy

Wishing the ceiling was the floor

Picking out massed produced bouquets made of silent disappointments sung aloud

You don't hold me anymore

I need you to fill my bouquet and give me meaning

I need you to share my view

Stop wasting all your tomorrows on a person who gives away your todays

IN THE SMALLEST OF HOURS

Devoid of innocence does anyone see the darkest presence?

Eternal in its nakedness for which a blind man can even see

I wait for you

I wait in the starry skies

I wait in the blistery sun

I wait in the seasons where the autumn colors genesis to green pastures

I'm not sure if you're going to answer, I honestly don't even remember if I'm alive

Feeling a foot succumbing to the trappings of the mouth of a darker place

I'm watering for what feels like nothing

The need persists

In the smallest hours, acceptance defeats darkness

Even in the smallest hours

Jonathan Faia

KEROUAC

I grew up with a mind engulfed

Being lost in a sense of Kerouacian dreams

No punctuation or structure, just raw thought traveling at its own pace

Surrounded by many but left to bloom alone

Until I've said it all I won't be free

I was convinced that we all live without knowing

Knowing anything about who we are could only mean the end

Hoping to love more than we lost

Praying for the answers in life to come in spontaneous prose

My shortcomings are not my passions, but my lack of control over them

LEAVE IT BEHIND

Regret is the dream that left you stained

Hearing names, so many things come to mind

Memories overtaken by smells, feelings, and visions

I can't keep but holding on to the very essence of your mind

The very being of you

I never just reduced you to an appearance, I saw deeper than that

I swam in the depths of you

You had magic in your veins and hope in your heart

You're everything I couldn't leave behind

Jonathan Faia

LIFT OFF

Your heart is packing a suitcase for the Sun

I will never mistake the colors you painted the world or the impression you left on my soul

You remind me that you've held on as long as you could to someone who didn't deserve your grip

You've lost enough sleep thinking about someone who didn't deserve to be on your mind

Continue to show the ability to feel unconditional, it makes you beautiful

You won't believe it today, but in time you'll be surprised with a love that mirrors your own

One day I'll find the right words and they'll be simple

When we fight, you'll be fighting with someone who chooses to fight for you

Until then be strong and rise from the ashes, leave behind those who wish you to fail

Take the prayers in your heart and use them because they're stronger than the words of your enemies

It's time to take your crown

LUCKY MAN

I want to share your breath and be your dream

The love of your life

Your fairytale

Just as you were and always have been mine

I have no accomplishment that will ever be greater than you

You save me

You create me

You've been my only light

Your love is the merry go round I never want to stop

You are everything that led me to believe

You are the wonder in all I see

I want you to know, I've always loved you and held you high above me

I see your face and my fears go away

Jonathan Faia

THE GREATEST VIEW

She lived unusual, banked with rose-colored thorns

She was both milk and honey

Waiting for me her love was casual, but with her I was complete

Her thoughts were the Sun to me

She comforted me when the candles went out

Her absence was my neon ghost

LIFE IN COLOR

My psalms don't read like a diary or speech

They're pictures made of words

IN HIDING

I want you to know, I love the way you laugh

With a whisper you broke into my imagination

Whatever is there is yours to take

KASHMIR

Soft midnights blessed in Kashmir

I'm a loser at the top of my game

My heart has become empty, a hotel full of rumors

Still chasing your stars made of amethyst

While the rains continue to drink champagne, I hide in rumination

Applauding my empty room

Waiting on a memory

SPRING

I love how you leave your daydreams out for anyone to find

It allows the wind to pick them up and spread them like seeds in the Spring

I was lucky enough that the breeze blew your dreams in my direction

PAUSE

I pause for birds because like love, the Sparrow is immortal

Jonathan Faia

BETWEEN

I still spend heartbeats trying to find the parts of me left hidden between the pages

COLLISION

When does the part come when I get to put myself back together again?

You know, the part where I tell you everything is okay while pretending not to fall apart

Starving for merit I'm left screaming in rescue

Everything breaks once

SERMON

It's a complicated blessing

Everything reminds me of her

Her silhouette is impaled on my soul

She's my Sun, my steeple

TRY NOT TO BREATHE

In rhythmic quietude, let me show you how it feels to love with your eyes closed

KING'S CROSSING

It's funny when you hurt so bad all you want is not to feel

You dream about how much better it would be to feel nothing at all

Then the medication kicks in, and you get your wish

You're void of all emotion and you long for the days when you at least felt something

No highs or lows, just a dry plain where invention used to be

BARSTOW

How bright is too bright?

Was it bright enough to see her soul?

The answer was yes, but eternity sounded better

Barstow became an empty heaven that night

There were no more words

No rocking horse in time

Just a stuttering goodbye

WESTCHESTER

I'm still here

Sitting amongst the Judas Decembers

Scratching the word survival in my arm

You pretended we were the same to make me feel normal

The truth was I was so much worse

Wielding silence like a hammer, I want you to know I'm trying

I promised myself I'd only think of you with a smile

Perpetually reliving our Mockingbird afternoons

That goodbye is still my carrion

APOLOGIES

I've spent most of my life anchored in hope

I wanted to be your stitches, but most days I was the wound

Jonathan Faia

SAILING

Living has taught me more about loss than it ever has about belonging

Learning the hard way that not everything in life that grows, must be watered

The love you give becomes a one-way mirror of reaction

Every page I attempt to write is empty, pining for lost poems and late-night promises

I wear your goodbye as if it was my definition

WELCOME HOME

If only life could move in soft subtle sighs

Wistful and without anger

The world's words weigh nothing until spoken from your mouth

Jonathan Faia

SOMETHING IN THE AIR

Aren't we all looking to be saved?

Second only to looking to be loved

Somewhere inside me there's a love song

The kind you listen to in the dark, when the deepest part of your heart aches

All that being said, I don't like the feeling of being me

SIMPLE DAYS

Stark visions mean nothing without words of possibility

Jonathan Faia

LOW

With a head full and overflowing with conceit

Love can make you low

It can become your humility

It becomes your one breath, shunning the World's disbelief

Only finding residence in faith

Finding a homeland in the certainty of one single sigh

STATIC LULLABY

I've spent a lot of life thinking about writing, but not getting much done

Sometimes, I just don't have the strength

I guess the same goes for life

Some days you get stuck trying to remember if you said goodbye to the Sun or not

Did you thank the wind, the grass, and every other semblance of beauty that you found in your own disgrace?

Blessing trees in your black aperture

Taking time to say goodbye to the faces known best, and to the ones you didn't have the chance to greet

Goodbye to the things that haunted your sleep, and to all your ideas that somehow were conceived out of fear

I never took the time to speak enough about the lives I'd be leaving behind, or the life I'm leaving incomplete

In case I run out of time you should know your smiles were the reason that I held on so long

Life can be so opaque that it's hard to find peace

Printed in the United States
by Baker & Taylor Publisher Services